You ARE Here

Dawn Lanuza

Andrews McMeel
PUBLISHING®

Also by Dawn Lanuza

The Last Time I'll Write About You
The Boyfriend Backtrack
What About Today
The Hometown Hazard
Break-Up Anniversary

To Phoebe,
May flowers always
bloom on your day.

how it starts

how to love in the dark

No one knows how to love me when I'm sad
and I can't blame them for that
I don't even know how to love me
when the voices come at night
I hate and hate and hate
even when I fight.

No one knows how to love me when I'm mad
and I can't blame them for that
I don't even know how to stop me
when my voice gets loud
I hate and hate and hate
even when I muffle the sound.

No one knows how to love me
the way I am learning now
it takes time and patience,
tears and self-doubt
I hope and hope and hope
someone will come around.

What a whiny,
self-absorbed girl.
She thinks the worst of herself
when no one even cared
to say a thing or two at all.

all this wanting

I know about wanting.
I wanted a lot of things.

As a child, I wanted to have
a life-sized baby doll
feed it
bathe it
comb its hair
I saw it on TV, and I
wanted it
wanted it
wanted it.

As a teenager, I wanted to meet
this rock band
watch backstage
go on tour
fall in love with the man
I heard their song on the radio and I
wanted it
wanted it
wanted it.

Right now, I wanted to be
with you
catch shows on Friday nights
play football
shop for records
drive around at midnight
watch those shows on your couch
ruffle your hair
touch your face
kiss you good night and I
want it
want it
I want you so bad.

I know I said I know all about wanting
but I don't know a thing about having.

I haven't met you
but I already felt like
I was losing you

sad girl

The first boy she ever loved
told her she had sad eyes
but changed his mind quickly.
Instead, he called her eyes pretty.

She didn't know how to disagree:
take it back, 'cause see—
she was sad, she needed someone
to not call her reasons petty.

She didn't need the praise
he thought she required.
She needed company
as she learned to speak her mind.

Her sad eyes learned first
to say what she couldn't.
Isn't it sad that he couldn't stay
long enough to hear it?

the mechanic

You tinkered with this heart
made sure it worked fine
screwed back the falling pieces
before leaving it behind.

canceled plans

Didn't we talk about this?
We said we'd take on projects,
learn musical instruments,
take culinary classes,
write a goddamned book.
Well, I did the last bit.
The last I heard from you,
you started running in marathons,
the last thing I would've put on our "to-do list"
but hey,
we're no longer present in the future
we once imagined in the past.

the perfect plate

When I think of you
I recall silly things.
Glazed doughnuts,
chocolate chip frappé,
linguini carbonara.
Did I ever tell you that I hate carbonara?
But I eat it anyway.
I keep thinking,
It'll get better
just like you and me.
And maybe once I find that perfect plate
you and I will have the same fate.
We'll have better timing;
we'll finally be on the same page.

pass the message

And all I wanted was someone to tap
like in one of those games I played as a child
I didn't even need a grand gesture
I just wanted to

Feel a pulse to dance along to,
some skin to touch,
a warmth to embody
before I lift my hand

See the pressure roll off
watch it travel to abled arms
feel it say,

Don't worry, I've got your back.

bad kisser

I regretted kissing you;
it was just so bad.
I wish I could kiss you more and more
to rid us of the last one we had.

araneta

And isn't it funny how I used to kiss you on your lips?
Now I have to settle for your cheeks.

Isn't it funny how you used to ask me, "Stay, please?"
now I have to get in this cab and watch you leave.

And the boy who wanted her to stay
was one of the first ones who went away

imaginary futures

You've painted a nice future for me
one where I'm right by the sea
surrounded by books, drinking my tea.

I envisioned this future you imagined for me
one where I'm looking out the balcony.
The sky is blue, the horizon is endless.

I'm sorry, but how come you're not in this?

the breakup

Are we breaking up?
I haven't answered the question
but I could already see the strings snap,
watch the pieces of the puzzle fall out.

It was like standing in the middle of a museum
looking at the things we built in frames.
Nothing seemed wrong from afar
but we knew that the paint was chipping away.

Are we breaking up?
As if it were my decision.
You already did everything to make me
say yes to the question.

the museum of unfinished things

We painted these walls
with our stories
I'm watching the chips fall
crying

Weren't we building a masterpiece?
How come we're leaving it unfinished?

passing through

Missing you is a tidal wave,
it swallows me whole.
It reminds me of something bigger
than what I've settled for.

Your love is a vast ocean
with depths of still unknown.
I was accustomed to silent rivers,
lovers who simply tread along.

My heart had cracks,
it couldn't contain it all.
Your love went past me
and found a better home.

the new normal

Nothing's changed.
You still watch the same shows
listen to the same songs
wear the same clothes.
You just lost me, that's all.

you were my first draft

You accused me of holding back

even when
you had
all of my
unedited
parts

that is so last season

I wish you witnessed
the stars in my eyes
the rhyme in my voice
my heart on my sleeve
I rarely wore it
but with you, I did.

Shame you never saw it;
shame you never will again.

travelers

I was a substitute: someone you talked to while you got over someone you met before we did. I was the transition, how to pass time as you moved from point A to point B.

And I never knew how to keep people. I could never just hold on. Part of me always wants to go, to wander, to roam. But then— you were slipping away first.

So I made it into a competition, found you a replacement soon as you started to do the same. He was temporary—as expected— but you found someone more comfortable with the word *permanent*.

And while I would rather avoid watching you shower her with your affection like you did with me, I couldn't help but stare. We were in the same town. We run in the same circles. Every day, I felt a twinge turn into a pinch, until it was squeezing, draining, heart-wrenching.

I always thought, *But that was me, not so long ago.*

Despite telling myself that you were never the guy for me. You were a substitute, someone who showed up with bandages when my heart had scratches. You were the boost that I needed, all kind words and good intentions, but always wondering, curious, full of life.

See, I was never that girl for you.
I was just a tourist attraction.
But you were that guy for me.
You've always been my go-to destination.

There are a thousand ways
to say I miss you but
I could never just
let those words
roll off of my tongue
to get the job done

I was here

I picked that shirt that you were wearing
in this photo that you were showing.
Your eyes were blue and smiling,
next to this girl that you were dating.

It made me smile that a part of me was there
even when you obviously didn't care.
It was my own version of scribbling, *I was here*.
Even if it was just with who you once were.

self-medicate

One pill down
here we go
that takes care of the pain
in my head, so

Two nights in
don't you know
I've been living in this bed we shared
thinking of you, oh

Three words then
never heard you say them again
you replaced one with the other
and didn't even bother

Two nights in
since you left the scene
never saw your face again
where did you go?

One pill down
another one, another one
I do this to numb the pain
but it's never done

falling in love with your words

They told me
those were just words;
don't rely on them completely.
But don't they know?
All we had were our words.

We fell
madly
completely
blindly
in love with our words.

We said
what we said
because we believed.

We heard
what we wanted
because of what we perceived.

Belief is a funny thing
hope is a wonderful feeling
trust, it seems,
is the only thing lacking.

the one thing I missed the most

The one thing I missed the most were his lips,
the way they would part and stretch from the sides
but then again,
it was his smile.

That brief moment of joy that bubbled up from his being
the very thing I wanted most about him.
Happy, he was my image of it,
bright sunflowers in a field of green.

But what of his words?
Carefully chosen syllables
radiating kindness and grace
it always brought a smile upon my face.

to the one I wanted to marry, on your wedding day

Cheers, darlin'
this is a pretty great night
for those who didn't know me
I was the girl before the bride.
Not here to cause trouble
I just wanted to be a part
of this dream I had
when I was still around.
That was a pretty good track
to walk on the aisle with, by the way.
I would have picked a different tune for the bride
but then again,
this is her wedding day.

she wins

All I have
are these words
my written prose

Now she's got
all your words,
your attention,
your affection,
your tomorrows.

this is our cosmos

We have these things,
our little inside jokes.
A whole library of facts collated
passed on by a knowing look.

We have these things,
a glimpse of the world
created by faithful companions
before we slipped back to our own.

Why do you always put me through the motions of
losing you
when all along you knew
that I never really had you?

off with your head

"You didn't need to write about that," you said.
That was your death sentence.

And what if she doesn't return,
what if you lose sight of the girl?

how it bends

The thing is—
you can end your life
but lives will carry on:
babies will be born
flowers will still bloom
books will be written
songs will be sung.
The Earth will complete its revolution.

You're the only one missing out,
not them.

Not all
heartbreaks
have to end
with you
broken.

this is your lullaby

It's okay
if you find yourself
sitting by the fridge
bawling your eyes out

If it caught you upright
and you had to lie down
in the middle of the room
to cry your heart out

It's okay
if it happens to you
in the middle of the night
when no one is watching

It's okay.
You're okay.
You can wear your sadness
at midnight.

You can keep crying
til you fall asleep.
As long as you're hurting,
it's okay.

You're okay.
You're gonna be okay
in the morning.

start of the week

Why is the start of the week always hard?
Is it the idea of starting over,
of putting the mask back on
of hiding the safety pins that held you together
and the backstitches that covered your gapes and holes?

Is it because you have to stand up straight
until you get to the end,
until you crawl back to bed
take the mask off
let your insides spill?

You're a mess;
no one needs to know it.
You're a mess,
until the start of the week.

crash and burn

There's excess in her heart
a loaded sigh
a river of tears
a heavy feeling

Where it came from
she doesn't know
she just feels it
in tiny doses

Sometimes she feels
sometimes she doesn't
when it comes she gets
thrown off her rocket

Sometimes she feels
sometimes she wished she didn't.

And isn't it sad
to be sad
and not be able to say it

true nightmare

You don't feel safe in yourself anymore
terrified of doing something
uttering a single thing
you can't recover from

Nothing's scarier than not knowing
what midnight brings
you pray to the gods
even if it sounds like wishful thinking
You scare yourself more than
anything,
anyone.

You're the darkness,
desperately seeking moonlight.

misfit

Sometimes you just wake up
and the world still feels all right
it's just that:
You're the odd one out.

role-playing

Don't cry yet
it's too early in the evening
you've got roles to play
you should be all dressed up
bright and beaming.

When it's over
hang your clothes to dry
and get in the shower,
the water will muffle your cry
and tap you on your shoulders:

You did well, love.
Now surrender.

breaking waves

I feel it coming like the waves of the ocean.
Sometimes it's calm,
sometimes it's a current.

I feel it coming, looming in my chest
darkness growing inside
spreading to my arms and legs.

Living with this for years
taught me how to look for signs,
listen to the sound of my bones and insides.

My mind is aware,
I make it in time;
I swim back to shore,
I save my mind.

Yet sometimes I know
and I still couldn't.
I feel myself let go,
I just drown in it.

good news / bad news

You've finally stopped falling asleep to your own tears
You close your eyes and nothing appears
When you dream, that's when you wake
You open your eyes and find your pillows stained

roller coaster

I don't know what to tell you—
some days it gets better
some days it feels like
it all fell apart

Some days would get so good
you doubt you were ever at the bottom
'cause how could it be this good, right?
You must have imagined it all now

But some days it gets so bad
that you forget all the good days you had.
You doubt you'd ever get one again
and is it even worth holding out?

When people say life is a roller coaster
we all think, *Oh, how fun!*
But we forget just how horrible it was
to hold your breath
close your eyes
anticipate that drop

And yeah you'll feel a high
a certain adrenaline rush
but can you imagine living life like that?

Being strapped in a roller coaster of your emotions
and you just want to get out
but your seat belt's tucked tight
and the ride just won't stop.

sometimes you just need
someone else's arms
to keep you intact

while

you

were

breaking.

only if you must

If you must leave her,
leave her without stepping on her toes.
Don't bruise her lips
and silence her words.

If you must leave her,
tip her chin up
and turn away slow.
Better keep her head up as you go.

"She could take care of herself,"
doesn't mean she didn't need someone else to do it.

bencoolen

You're in a different city
lying on a different bed
you're still crying
underneath all these threads.

The rush of the day
the sights, the sounds
worked for you in the daylight
but left you by night.

You're still you:
a hollow shell,
a brook babbling,
a mountain erupting,
silently,
patiently.

Put a lid on the crater
and still the lava flows
mad, angry lines spilling:
your temporary fixes are failing.

passengers

Sometimes you see people with the same look,
the one you've been trying to fix in front of the mirror
in the morning,
at night.
They look so lost and confused
that you want to take out
pieces of paper you kept in your bag, your pockets.
Maybe you can all pick it apart and compare
your notes, lessons
like unfolding an old map to answer
How do I get here?
Which way do I go?
What's the fastest route possible?

maps

If you found yourself lost
and can't seem to turn back
consider that—
you're not supposed to turn around.

Keep moving forward.
Tread along the path even if it's dark.
Maybe where you were
isn't where you're supposed to be,
and who you were
isn't who you're supposed to be
now.

honey sweet

Some people grew up with honey in their tongues
their words sound sweet,
an antidote to doubts.

I barely seek your words
because I was terrified
you are pure nectarine
it could get addicting, fast.

I wish I could keep you,
let you speak nice.
My ears are leaking blood
from scratching poison off my mind.

When you leave, I
try to savor the sweetness
but I always run out.
I know I shouldn't keep you
but can you please keep coming back?

staying is your choice

It's not that you don't fall in love
you do
in fact
you fall in love with people
who made you laugh
who made you think.
You even fall in love with people
just for their smiles
or how they talk.
You fall in love,
you do
but falling in love
and staying in love
are two different things

Perhaps you have not learned
to stay

Perhaps you've yet to find
a good reason to

come home

When did you decide that you were
too small for a love that is enormous?

Who gave you the impression that your heart
is too tight to welcome a love so abundant?

You are an abandoned house,
waiting for the lights to turn on.
You are someone else's home.

you've got standards, so what?

Here comes another article
telling you why you're single
enumerating all the "wrong" things you've done.

You're too picky, it said.
Maybe it's true but
when you've been loved well,
would you ever settle for anything less?

the tale of the girl

They told the young girl,
"Be hasty, be wise.
Choose a man who'd give you
your best life."

The young girl grew
into a woman
so now they tell her:
"Be careful, be smart.
You can't afford to refuse
another heart."

When did the story change?
Why do we flip the script when women age?

to my younger self

There are people who would come for you
They'd celebrate your beauty and your youth
They will gawk and stare and suck you in
Hold yourself together, don't believe everything

There is a boy in another room
His eyes twinkle like the stars, the moon
His heart carries a love so immense
You weren't ready for it, so don't bend

There are people waiting for you
They will come and listen to your tune
They will pull words out of your mind
They feed your soul, keep you in line

There is a woman writing this for you
She's got regrets and scars from her youth
She's acquired a thicker skin, a better disposition
Most of all, she'd want to tell you,
You're forgiven.

snooze the alarm

What's life like
never fearing what
the weighing scale
tells you in the morning?

vessel

I see nothing wrong with my body
when I look at it in the mirror, naked.
In fact I think it looks quite lovely

That is until I get dressed
and look at my phone
then I start to wish for
a longer torso
a smaller waist
skinny arms and legs

Even worse is when I
look at my older photos
and wish I looked the same
completely forgetting about
how I got here,
how this body grew.
How it held me through the changes,
how it carried me through.

grow

At one point would you stop wishing
that you had a different nose
better hair
lighter skin
lips like a rose.

At one point would you know
that it's your job to learn
how to be enough
no, not for a man.

It's all for you.
It always has been.

let flowers bloom

I wish they didn't require us to acquire thick skin.
I wish they told us to grow tender hearts instead,
to let our tongues soften.

I wish we were raised to be kind,
not cruel
Then we would be carefree,
not careful.

warm lights, cold nights

Some nights I miss the city
miss that coffee shop near the stadium
miss getting breakfasts for dinner
miss staying out late scribbling words on paper
miss the dim yellow lights on the street
miss the noisy streets go quiet
miss seeing you, in a heartbeat
miss being where you are.

Some nights I miss the city
but I'm far better where I am now.

a message

And to you who thought that I have changed:
the truth is, I didn't.

I just learned how to speak
instead of remaining silent.
To not be afraid
of expressing my thoughts
when I used to be shamed for it.

And most of all I learned
how to treat myself better,
enough to expect others
to meet me at that level.

dead bolts

You're knocking on the door
realizing that it's closed
reaching up the jamb
lifting back the rug

Looking for the keys
that weren't there anymore
twisting the knob, calling my name
scratching on the surface.

Meanwhile I
stare at the door,
purse my lips
then turn my back.

I am done falling for that.

migratory birds, too

I watched you move
from continent to continent
looking for a better climate
escaping the cold.

Has it always been about
survival?
Has it always been about
protecting yourself?

Who made you believe that you were hard to love?

These days, whenever I start doubting my capability to feel,
I think of how it used to be with you—
and I remember.

I can.
I will.
At the right time.
With the right one.

citizen

And then sometimes
you wake up
to a world that is so
messed up,
you realize—
you're here for something,
someone,
so you get up.

rise

Once you reach the bottom
and feel yourself rise,
realize:
it really does get better—
not perfect,
maybe not even that great but
some days come with a great exhale.

Breathe in.
Then out.

Keep it up.

how it goes

a prelude

Every beginning
has an ending

Don't let the goodbye
scare you from starting
what could be
the best
story of your life

qualified

I've got a knot in my chest
that needed untangling
I require able hands
strong and willing,
careful and stirring,
patient and forgiving.
I need no retreat, no fumbling.

doomsday prepper

I am somewhere between
assuming someone out there
is meant for me and
preparing myself for the possibility:
this person doesn't exist.

the art of eating alone

I remember being nineteen and dreading the day that I had to eat in public alone.

Then I turned twenty-two and mastered the art of it.

I eat alone in a room filled with groups of people talking and laughing loudly. I hog a table and shut these people out with my earphones and submerge myself into the world of fiction. I never hurry in fear of people judging me. I linger, look out the window, laugh or frown, regardless of what people might think.

It was then that I learned to like my own company.

It is through this—the simple act of eating alone—that I am learning how to be my own.

nine lives

I think it's a mistake to tell us
we've only got one life.
By all means, make us believe
that we've got nine lives.

Like cats jumping on our rooftops,
maybe then we wouldn't be afraid.
And if we failed,
so what?

We can always start over again.

Let us believe that we can take chances,
retreat if we found ourselves in a dead end.
These lives we could have lived?
Let us live them.

the ideal

I imagine someone sitting across from me at this table with a
worn-out paperback in his hands. I peer into him while my
hand scribbles these words. He would slightly raise his head,
put the book down an inch or so, and reveal a smile that I
would return. We would remain silent, and we would not
feel the need to utter a word to check how the other is doing,
because we already know.

I would close this notebook, just as he would his book, and we
would stand up from our seats. He would put a hand around the
small of my back to lead me out, and we would leave the place
with nothing but a silent giggle or a mum smile.

All this time, I kept on telling people that I wanted someone
to have great conversations with. Someone I could stay up all
night talking to. And I still want that, but I also realized that,
above all things, I was looking for someone who I could be in
solitude with.

Someone I wouldn't mind tagging along with to things that I
usually love doing on my own.

Someone who wouldn't feel left out when I've gone missing,
imagining things in my head.

Someone who would listen to a song with me without talking
over the sound.

Someone who would join me in a library or a bookstore, scouring the bottom shelves.

Someone who could sit with me in silence without being afraid of what it all means.

One of life's simplest pleasures is witnessing someone smile at you for the first time.

when I said "nice to meet you," I meant

Meeting you is like
checking a list I didn't know I had.
You're pure magic but
here's the best part:
you're real,
not at all made up,
and you liked me just as much.

the band was surprisingly good though

Well, the music's loud
but I'm convinced that
we preferred to
let our cheeks touch

It's a secret language
a whisper, a rush
a whole world built
just for the two of us

Maybe for you I was
only part of the night
yet for me
you simply
made the night

imagine

I imagine to love you
the way I love my family and friends.
I would spend time to know you,
share meals, share beds.

I imagine to love you
the way I love my passions
I would examine your details
and study you for hours.

I imagine to love you
the way I never have.
A whole new world of possibilities
I'll only explore with you, love.

plans

I'm sure you've got your own history
I will learn it all

One day

But tonight
let's just stick
to your anatomy

I'm no artist

no critic

but darling,

you are a work of art.

double-edged swords

When I think of you
my mind latches to your memory
everything comes back to me
I'm the shore
you're the wave
you crash into me

I fill every crack with my longing
you stick with me til the wee hours of the morning
I recall the things you said to me
play it back til my eyes feel heavy

And in the morning, I
will taste your name on my lips
as I eat my breakfast
and drink my bitter coffee

Soon my mouth will forget
the taste of yours
and so will my skin
that is until I see you again

You are agony
and sanctuary,
just the way I like it to be.

that's something

This is how it starts, isn't it?

All the waiting.

For the person to get back to you.

For them to respond.

For when it's time to do the things that meant that you two are moving along.

You have done this, and now I do this.

Like a dance.

Right foot forward.

Left foot back.

If you've done this enough, the progression of things would seem like a natural occurrence.

If you're like me, who has taken a long hiatus, every little thing is a milestone.

Look, I said the first hi. That's something.

He kept asking me questions. That's something.

This conversation is still going on. That's something.

He said good night. That's something.

He said good morning.

How you've missed this, that's something.

And so the next day, you wait for your good morning, good night, and the in-betweens.

You wonder what other milestones you'd reach with him.

These are little things.

Maybe puny to some.
But for someone who is trying again,
they are monumental.

settling

How do you know,
how do you just know?
Do you just wake up one day,
decide to want it, and take it?

Or do you hold out?
Explore all the options,
run after vague ideas,
until you exhaust it all?

What if this was it,
just not wrapped in the way you imagined it?

You will never get to know
someone for the first time again
the same way that you can't
unread a book,
unhear a song,
unlearn a word.
Goodbye may be inevitable
but live through it all.

enough and never more

My head is always heavy
filled with all these worries
questions for tomorrows

I am empty
staring into my reflection, thinking,
I've got nothing left in my bones.

All of me is on paper
these impressions
memories of people who come and go

I am a monument
frozen in time
I am this human
incapable of growth

I wish to continue,
break free from it all
but they kept saying:

Stay this way,
everything is perfect,
don't rock the boat.

I am itching
driving myself mad
I need movement
I need action

I am a person
jumping up and down
I will lose things
in order to gain some.

I can't keep all of this,
my arms are sore.
I only need and will keep
what is enough and never more.

stop over

I did not talk to you today because I was feeling heavier than I normally do. I woke up on the wrong side of the bed, people might say; I was more exhausted than rested.

I felt like I had nothing to say, or I had no energy to sustain a conversation, so I removed myself.

But I knew.

I knew at some point I had to get back to you. Say something. At least say, "I'm here, I'm alive."

But I didn't. I couldn't find the energy to start. Or worse, to maintain a conversation that would sound like everything is all right.

You came back to me at the very last minute, before you close your eyes to say good night.

I felt bad because you were probably waiting for me to say something, like I thought, but I was too selfish to give you even the tiniest of warnings.

At some point, I may have to tell you that this happens to me. Occasionally.

I disappear.

I refuse company.

That seems like a bad thing to say, especially to a person you're trying to be with, but who am I kidding?

You're going to find out.

As a response, I asked you a question. "How was your day?"

You mentioned that you're not feeling very well; it must be your migraine. And so my instinct kicked in—I asked about your meds, told you to sleep it off, and hoped you'd feel better in the morning.

I didn't tell you about my sickness.

Unlike you, I don't have over-the-counter medicines.

I wish I could sleep it off, but I've done that before. It's either I sleep all the time or I don't sleep at all.

Sleep today seemed like surrender, and I still wanted to win, even if I was exhausted battling this whole day.

At some point I have to tell you.

If I want this to move forward, you have to know.

I just don't know when the best time is.

Do I tell you now, as a warning? So that before you proceed, you would know that I have this? It's not going away. It's not something I would miraculously snap out of.

Or do I tell you when I'm more comfortable talking about it? I don't know when that is, but maybe when I already feel safer telling you all of my flaws?

I couldn't decide.

Would I be issuing you a warning?

Or am I showing you a way in?

welcomed distractions

They first called you a distraction,
I didn't disagree.
You were very good at what you did

You were exactly what I needed
A rogue, throwing pebbles at my window
sneaking out and running away

I called you for nights not just because
you're a getaway
you were something to look forward to, at night
when the world is quiet

You came and made this wait called my life
a circus: messy, beautiful, and bright.
A celebration, a sense of right.

second loves are underrated

It shouldn't be compared to first love
but it can't be helped
second loves are so underrated in a way that
he was better at handling my heart.

Second lovers are careful
gentle, delicate
like unwrapping gifts with a soft hand
not with the kind of recklessness
we all once had.

Perhaps because all second lovers
also have bent and bruised hearts.

the cleaners

Sometimes it feels like stepping inside your house after you've had a party that night. It's all a mess with the cups and chairs and your hair's still sticking out on the side, but I've got the gallon of orange juice in my hands.

You have her written all over the walls, 'cause she's lived here, of course, with her clothes in the closet, her toothbrush hidden in the medicine cabinet. There are things that once belonged to her, tucked in these tiny corners that you might have missed that one time you cleaned, but I still don't move a thing.

I understand. This is your space, and all of your memories are yours: to keep, to clean.

But I will hand you that broom like I would pour you this glass of orange juice, to help rid you of this sick hangover you've been having.

y / n

Let's have the kind of love
that puts fires to shame.
We'll burn ever so brightly,
we'll tend to the flame.

Let's fall in love
like we never did before
or like we did
and learned from it all.

superman

He's no hero
he's just a man
but he did something amazing,
I'll tell you what:

He made living a delectable option
every day less of a burden.
She's started to envision a future
she never thought she'd have.

all I had was white space

Oh, how my life lacked color
until you came with cans of paint
and splashed it all over

You're a kaleidoscope,
a marvel, out of this world
and I am grateful.

waking up to a dream

In the morning
I will find you
wrapped up in a blanket
head turned to the side
sleeping like a child

In the quiet
I will find
that you are not the dream
I had when I was young

You are
the sum of all the desires
I picked up
as I walked through this life

You are
the lessons I learned
as a stubborn girl,
impatient and wild

You are
hope personified
when I cried myself
to sleep at night

You are
the promise,
the life I wanted,
the one I'm living now.

Loving someone is a hard climb as it is.
Allowing yourself to be loved—
is a much higher summit.

the tourist

This city is kind to strangers
but there is no magical land
especially when your sadness
is bound to your insides.

Oh, how you wished for this
back when you couldn't afford it.
You thought running away
would solve all the problems.

But you know better now,
and you are learning still.
No amount of change in the climate
could tame the storm in your head.

But this city is kind,
and the weather is cooler.
There is music in the streets,
and you can breathe better.

the doctor will see you now

Why is it hard to tell people that you hurt
if you can't point to a wound?
Or even a bruise,
a broken bone?

Why do we question the hurt,
even when we feel like bleeding,
especially when we feel broken?

the hunter and the haunted

It's so easy to come home to your unhealthy habits,
you can walk back to the fridge and wolf back its contents.
Have a whiff of a cigarette 'cause what's one hit?
Come out to prey on a lion who's hunting for the likes of you.

You're no deer, you've caught so many.

Spun them in a tangle of
yes and no
come and go
and when you're done you spit them out.

Look for a new one
until the game chokes you
turn your heart hard or soft?
You can't tell anymore.

But at times you go back and seek that life,
prey on the hunter 'cause you wanna see what it's like
to be the one surrendering,
letting go of control.

But these are monsters,
just like you,
out to steal your soul.

excess baggage

I majored in you for the past few years
specialized on your habits and quirks
now I'm out into this world
armed with this knowledge

But tell me,
what do I do with this?
How do I go about carrying
all of these bits?

Sometimes when I feel like
a part of me is missing or lacking
I wonder: whatever did you do
with the pieces I left with you?

Look at all these places
I've never been
next to you

projection

And maybe she's asking for too much
she wanted stability
but couldn't keep in touch

How can she expect someone to keep her
if she can't even get ahold of herself?

I'm always at the brink of holding on
and letting go,

of *I need to talk to you*
and *Please leave me alone*

diagnosis

They told me I have chronic pain,
so I looked it up.
It said, *Any pain lasting more than 12 weeks.*
I laughed because
I have been in pain for way longer than that.
In fact parts of me started to feel numb.
So what do you call that?

sylvia

All you have are painkillers
but did you ever stop?
You googled *How to overdose on ibuprofen*,
and it seemed like you weren't the only one.

Sylvia took some sleeping pills
but they only thought her missing.
She slept for three days
before they found her still breathing.

Your search results came:
How to not kill yourself.
Not through this, then.
Not this way.
Not today.

therapy sessions

Tonio with the hairline fracture on his hand was being treated next to me. It had been so for three days when he started talking to me about his son. He told me he missed him and how he regretted not seeing him grow up due to a separation from his wife. I sat there tight-lipped, nodding off my sympathies because I am not like him, who talks about these things so openly to strangers, at least not face-to-face.

Tonio, with his hands dipped with once-hot wax, asked me how old I was. I thought for a minute that he would ask me to go see his son but—

Tonio, who looked about sixty or so, who fell on his back and used his hand to soften the fall, then told me that his son died at twenty-seven. He thinks of him often, of his son's dreams that didn't come true, of the life he didn't get to live through.

I sat there, thinking:

I'm clinging to my last days of twenty-eight
I used to know a boy who was older than me by forty-eight days, but
Now I keep adding years to my life
While he remained twenty and seven
Young and eternal,
Six feet under the earth, and

I have pain shooting up to my head and neck, stretching onto my
shoulders, my arms, my hands
All of my fingers are numb
I don't know how I'll be able to keep working at this rate
And do I have to?
But how do I keep living?
And then I thought,
Maybe from here on out, this is what it means to keep living:
to carry on with injured parts
and tattered hearts and
the years
just
keep
on
piling
up

It's a daunting task to keep showing up
to settle into a routine or to shake things up,
which then, really, makes me want to question:

Are my dreams worth this much?
Is my life big enough?

ode to march

You had me screaming for medicine,
tugging at my sheets
because reality was crashing
and I was falling

a

p

a

r

t

Every fragment,
every word is a
symptom,
a side effect—
sometimes it dresses up
like identical twins
in stripes of black and white
running in my backyard

But

Some days I stumble upon
some kind of medicine:
sunlight,
melody of a new favorite song,
coming home.
Finding something new to love
that is in a way, my own.

Compliments,
changing my mind,
because I am allowed.

Then the fact that still remains:

I am alive.

not ready

And if you meet him—
tell him I'm sorry.
I'm sorry I never went
out of my way to meet him.

Tell him I wanted to meet him
but I was always afraid.

Tell him I see him
and the life we could have lived.
Tell him, *tell him*
I would have loved the shit out of him.

And I'm sorry,
so sorry,
because I wasn't able to.

Tell him I believed in him
and in the promise of a better life.
I believed in our first dance,
fireworks, and fairy lights.

I believed in him,
of his goodness,
his existence.
I believed that he would come.

But tell him I'm sorry,
as much as I have faith in him,
I have none for me.

It is probably why
it's taken this long
for us to stay apart.

idol / idle

He bleached his hair blond,
shaved it to one side.
They said he's looking fit
wearing those tight jeans.

His frown has gone permanent,
kept his eyes down at times.
His voice sounded the same
but his words fell flat.

He's present, tangible,
a living god walking around.
But the more he stayed on stage
the more he faded out.

Like the weight he lost,
the hair he shaved,
the light from his eyes
has disappeared.

Every day he was losing a piece of himself,
yet this was everything he wanted
in his old life.

He's grown up
and grown out of it.

youth, it's painful

And maybe if he waited a little longer
he wouldn't have to lose so much
but he's young and therefore braver
than the rest of us.

touché

I wanted to keep you so much that
I broke a piece of you
to keep for myself

I've been holding on to you
with clenched hands—
now,
look at all this blood.

3x5

And here is my heart
riding on a 3x5
there's no need to say hello.

I'll just get straight to the point:

I miss you.
I wish we never let go.

a plea

You have to understand
the proper response to
"I can't do it anymore" is not
"What did I do wrong?"

How hard can it be to just ask,
"How can I make it easier?"
"How can I help you?"

Don't forget how good I was
in case I forget.
I always seem to do it.
Remind me every once in a while,
I might need it
that one time.

resolutions

Taking things leisurely means
not ordering things on the go,
not eating on the road anymore,
not *not* eating at all,
I'm going to take a seat and savor a meal, that's all.
I'm not going to kill myself little by little anymore.

selfish

Allow me to be selfish these days.
You're leaving and I've only got
sixty-something days.

I don't want to burden you
with questions like,
Who do I go to when I'm running away?

See, I knew we'd grow up
but I always thought
together we'd grow old.

But growing up takes
some people apart.
I'm not naive but—

Soon we will be oceans apart.

Allow me to be selfish this time around.
I'd like to still have you in my life,
the way it has been,
before you board that flight.

I'm torn between deciding whether or not life is cruel.
On one hand, it brought me you

Yet it kept me from having you.

it is not mine

It is not mine. I can make it so, but it is not mine.

When it is yours, you'll feel the hurt.
You will feel the need to make it so.
You will ache until you hold it.
And sometimes even more when you already have it,
because it is yours to keep and lose.

But sometimes, the hardest thing to do is to let go of
what is not yours.

You're not a secret,
you're one of my favorite tales to tell.
Like a bedtime story, I remind myself
that every once in a while,
miracles do happen.

I still
write about
you
sometimes

a silent prayer

I'm in no hurry
I won't worry
I'll come to this page and think,
This is my medicine
watching the sand fall from that opening
biding my time

No one is after me
no bill
no child
no man
I dictate when to have
what I want to have in my life

I'm in no hurry,
I won't worry.
Things will play out
right when it's time.

She was lost
but she never returned,
didn't retrace her steps
and just carried on.

She built herself a new home.

seasons

You've already started
to water yourself with goodness
expected your buds to bloom
only to prune them before they had the chance,
and denied yourself sunlight.

You have so many seasons to see,
don't let this winter stay longer than it has to be.
Look forward to your spring,
of sunflowers and sunshine.

Dance in the summer
and slow down at fall,
ride through your winter
without cutting ties or issuing last calls.

Some nights will be colder
but you will survive,
you always did
as long as you tried.

Let yourself go through all of this,
without guilt and shame.

Of course, you can love again.

One day you'll be brave again
to want something like this
and when that day comes
you'll be better equipped with the belief:
you deserve all the love,
you deserve all the happiness.

This is how it starts,
how it bends,
how it goes.
May you welcome it.

Dear Reader,

You have reached the end of this book. I previously released some of these poems in a chapbook called *This Is How It Starts*, working with the idea of giving oneself a second chance for a second love. But over time it grew and ultimately resulted in this very book.

As a romance writer, I write happily ever afters—and it's not an easy task. How to get there, and how to make the characters believe that they deserve love, always seemed to be a challenge.

I also struggle with this in real life. *You Are Here* is a testament to that.

This Is How It Starts ended with a happy ending, but sometimes it doesn't last. And that is also all right. I'd like to think that we are all on our way to affirming and reaffirming to choose happiness: in endings, beginnings, and in-betweens.

Lots of times we will feel lost, but I hope you trust your journey. You will meet people along the road: some will walk with you til your next destination, while some have different routes to go. Some even have shorter journeys than you.

You define what happily ever after means. It might change as you go about your way, and that's okay. You are allowed to change your mind, to want things you didn't want before, and vice versa.

Wherever you are in your path, I hope you remember to be kind to others, but most importantly to yourself. I am grateful that my book has crossed paths with you. Now go on your own way, as I must go mine. Let's meet each other again sometime.

Keep walking,
Dawn

NOTE

Some pieces made it here from my self-published chapbook,
This Is How It Starts:

all I had was white space
all this wanting
canceled plans
crash and burn
excess baggage
falling in love with your words
I'm no artist
I'm torn between deciding whether or not life is cruel.
imagine
Maybe for you I was
the mechanic
Not all
One day you'll be brave again
passing through
the perfect plate
plans
a prelude
second loves are underrated
staying is your choice
superman
that is so last season

There are a thousand ways
this is our cosmos
this is your lullaby
to the one I wanted to marry, on your wedding day
waking up to a dream
warm lights, cold nights
when I said "nice to meet you," I meant

y / n

You're not a secret
you've got standards, so what?

About the Author

Dawn Lanuza writes contemporary romance and young adult fiction. This is her second poetry collection. She has two first loves—music and writing—and is lucky enough to surround herself with them.

She currently lives with her adopted cream toy poodle.

Contact her at:

www.dawnlanuza.com
hello@dawnlanuza.com
www.facebook.com/AuthorDawnLanuza
Twitter: @dawnlanuza

my love and gratitude go to:

#romanceclass, for the love and confidence.

everyone who read and loved *This Is How It Starts*

Layla Tanjutco

April Cauilan

Reginald Lapid

Carla De Guzman

Patty Rice and the Andrews McMeel Publishing
team, for working diligently on this one.

Maan

Jay

Kara

Marie

My sister and her family, for providing
me shelter during the storm.

The Auckland Central City Library, for giving me the
space, literally and figuratively, to work on this.

My dog, who has been the most loyal
companion and the best cheerleader.

My family, friends, and kind strangers, who have offered
me support and showered me with goodness and love.

To all the places I've visited while I was working on *You Are Here,* thank you for letting me discover and rediscover you.

To the people who took a chance on *The Last Time I'll Write About You* and made it here, too: thank you for believing in me.

Lastly, to the people who have created the music that I listened to, whispered the words of affirmation and assurance that I needed while I go through the night: may my words reach you and give you comfort, too.

stay a little longer

Elan wasn't supposed to meet Caty. She lived halfway around the world, and he barely left Manila. Yet here he was, giving her a ride to the airport. Convinced that they would never have to see each other again after that day, Elan and Caty started to bond over truths, dares, stolen kisses, and games in hotel rooms and bars.

They were perfect strangers—all perks, no strings.

Until they weren't.

With brief encounters that turned them from acquaintances to friends—tipping to the point of lovers, *always*—will Elan and Caty keep settling for a day, or will someone finally dare to stay long enough to discover: is this is love?

Coming May 2019. Enjoy this sneak peek.

PART ONE

"Something has given my poor warm life
Into the hand of someone random
Who doesn't know what even yesterday I was."

RAINER MARIA RILKE

one—

It had been a long ride. Elan had ridden a bus for hours to the small town of San Juan to get his car. Normally, he found public transportation troublesome, but the moment he saw his friend Jules opening the gate for him, he stopped feeling antsy. Not even a bit unsettled.

He was just thankful.

And pathetic, because that guy waiting by the door was obviously the reason why Jules suddenly left the city as fast as she could. That's how Elan's car ended up in this driveway. That's why he was here in this town.

How had he ended up on the outside, while she was here with someone else? Well, Elan knew he'd had it coming. He'd seen her every day for the last few years but never made a move.

"I'm so sorry." She started apologizing as soon as she spotted him crossing the street toward the gate. It was an impressive gate. It screamed, "Rich people live here; don't even think about robbing it."

"I was supposed to ask someone to drive it back for you, but I—"

"Honestly, Jules," Elan replied as she took a step toward him. "It's alright. We're still on vacation, remember? It's nice to get out of the city for a bit."

Lie. Having grown up in the city, Elan wasn't used to small towns. He and his friends had flown to Bali a couple of weeks ago, but he had ended up feeling even more anxious. He needed his life to be on schedule, and sitting by the beach for hours, no matter how beautiful it was, only made him think of how much time was passing by.

"Well." Her eyes darted to the other guy waiting by the door. Elan followed her gaze and took in the other man—his competition, so to speak—but it looked like he'd already won.

The guy walked toward them with a small smile on his face. To be polite, Elan guessed. He knew that smile only too well. He'd used it on many occasions throughout his life.

The guy stopped, still a step away from Jules, and nodded at Elan. "Hey, man."

He nodded back. "Sorry. Was I early?"

It did look like they'd just gotten up—eyes glazed, hair messy, clothes wrinkled. But it was almost noon. Was that usual for small towns?

Jules finally spoke up: "Kip, this is Elan."

The guy nodded again, as if he recognized his name. He extended his hand, and Elan took it. "Sorry 'bout the car. We were going to take it back, but everything's just been hectic with the move."

Elan shook his head. "Don't worry about it."

Jules sighed, "I owe you so much, seriously. Have you had breakfast yet?"

Of course he had.

She checked her watch, rolled her eyes. "I meant lunch! We should get something ordered—"

"I'd love to, Jules," Elan interrupted. "But I actually need to get back today."

That wasn't a lie. He needed to get back because he had errands early tomorrow and he needed his car.

"Well," she took a deep breath. "Thank you so much for lending it to me again. I promise, whatever you want—name it—I'll make sure you get it."

Kip raised an eyebrow, hiding a knowing smile as he took a sip of coffee. She cleared her throat. "I mean, as long as it's reasonable."

Elan raised his hand to get the keys, and Jules obliged, dropping them squarely into his palm. He walked over to the car, giving her another look before opening the door.

"Wait!" he heard someone scream.

Elan looked around and saw a girl running out of the house, dragging a huge suitcase behind her.

She was looking at him, so she must have wanted him to wait for her.

He stood there, one hand on the door handle, mouth slightly agape, as she approached him.

The first thing he noticed was her lips. Bright and red and full. Then there was her hair, jet black and slightly unruly after the run. She was tall and quite intimidating, especially with her eyes covered by huge, dark sunglasses.

"I'm coming with you," she announced. Like this had been discussed. Like this was supposed to happen. Like he shouldn't say no.

He sucked in a breath, glancing back at Jules for an introduction or a confirmation, but the girl was already talking. "Excuse me. Hey you, sir, could you open up your trunk, please?"

Jules only smiled at him nervously. So Elan did what he did best: he put on a smile and agreed. He walked over and helped the girl with her suitcase.

"Oh God." Caty folded and unfolded her legs. She'd been shifting in her seat for the last fifteen minutes. She felt uncomfortable sitting next to a guy she didn't know.

What was his name again? Last night they mentioned he was coming to pick up his Jeep. He was a classmate from law school or something. He didn't look like a lawyer or even someone who'd be one soon. She still found it weird that people her age could be called lawyers. For the longest time, she thought that was a job for old and boring men.

This guy did not look old at all. He looked like the kind of guy you knew in high school but didn't get to know, because he liked to sit in a corner, all quiet and brooding. You wouldn't really notice him until the growth spurt finally kicked in. He would be the one who shocked everyone during the reunion, the little underdog. He just had that look about him. He was attractive but obviously didn't know how much or cared to inquire. He also had the most interesting nose—slightly crooked on the bridge, like it was broken in a brawl or a tackle. It gave the impression that he was more dangerous than he intended.

Yet he had his shirt all tucked in, hair trimmed neatly. He looked like the nicest boy in town.

Only he hadn't looked at her since he started driving, and he hadn't said one word. She wasn't sure if he was shy or just unapproachable.

This was the most uncomfortable drive she'd ever been on, and that included the ride she once shared with a woman whom an ex-boyfriend was currently seeing. *With the ex-boyfriend in the same car.*

She cleared her throat, assessing her situation: she was about to fly back to Toronto. Her parents had just sold her childhood home, and she didn't want to be too emotional about it. After all, San Juan wasn't her home anymore. She'd been away since moving to Toronto about a decade ago.

"So, you're Juliana's friend, right?" Caty started, figuring that he wouldn't talk unless she did.

He paused. "Yeah, Jules."

Jules. How chummy. She'd been a friend of Juliana's since they were babies, but she was never just *Jules.*

"Thanks for giving me a ride, by the way," she said, getting that out of the way. "I'm glad to finally get out of there, you know?"

266

His eyebrows furrowed.

She felt the need to explain. "Not that it isn't great. It is. My brother and my best friend. *Together.* That's, like, a porn story line."

He swerved right about the time she said that last bit, and it was too funny to watch him try and recover. He let out a nervous laugh and bit his lip as if to stop himself from showing emotion.

It would have worked, she thought, if it were someone else she knew better. It was an icebreaker of sorts, a funny ha-ha comment that should have relieved the awkwardness. But not with a complete stranger, and not in the Philippines, where sex is not something you talk about with a person you've only just met. Also, *porn* was definitely a taboo word.

Great, she'd made it more awkward.

Caty looked away, wincing at herself. "Sorry, wrong thing to say."

She didn't see how he reacted, didn't even hear a response. There was still a lot of time left before they reached their destination, and the silence was annoying. It would have helped if there were music in the background, but the radio wasn't on either. It was just so . . . quiet.

Caty glanced at him. "Well, we're stuck together now. We have to talk about something."

"And porn's the first thing that came to mind?"

Her eyes slanted. "Like sex isn't something you think about."

He licked his lower lip and bit back a smile.

Really, what did she have to do to make this guy even grin? She frowned and itched to ask him why he was so poor at handing out smiles and eye contact. Granted, they were strangers, but they were currently sharing a space and could at least be polite.

But maybe he already was being polite to her. She had asked him for a favor by giving her a ride. She decided to pull back. "I didn't mean like you give off a creepy vibe. You don't. We can just talk about, I don't know, how old this car is."

He snorted as soon as the word *old* left her mouth and didn't say anything back.

Alright, Caty thought. *This guy is stuck up. He couldn't possibly have been offended by that.* She was just really curious. Her father had taught her to like cars, and she knew the older ones often had interesting histories.

She clicked her tongue and took off her sunglasses, his silence starting to make her feel bad about what she'd just said, even though she hadn't meant for it to come off that way. She racked her brain for something else to say, but really, he should be the one to break the silence so she could stop saying the wrong things.

Yet he just sat there, focused on the road. *This guy can't be so boring,* Caty thought. *After all, he's Juliana's friend.* From what she could gather, Juliana liked him, but they didn't date or fool around.

That's Juliana. She was mostly anti-fooling around, even when they were kids. She liked rules and wanted things to be in order.

Caty tried again. "Okay, since we are driving all the way to the airport, you can pick the topic. I'll bite."

She sensed his hesitation. His arms stiffened as he squeezed the steering wheel. If he hadn't been so focused on being uninterested in socializing, she would have thought he was really cute.

Then, "Fine. I suppose you can tell me about your childhood."

She paused. "Wow."

"Wow?"

"Wow," Caty repeated. "That's very first date-y. Or not even. At least the third date."

"You have to wait for a third date to talk about your childhood?"

"Yeah," Caty nodded. "Third date's the time to decide if you're gonna keep seeing the dude. He passed the impression test on the first date, and let's face it, the second one is a do-over. Just to make sure he's really cute without the beer goggles on."

She slowed down, watching his reaction. His eyebrows raised then knitted. He didn't smile, but, boy, did his eyes talk.

"Beer goggles," he repeated, saying that a little bit slower. "What kind of first dates have you been having?"

"Fun ones," she replied. "And don't judge, Judy."

He snorted. He thinks that's funny? But it was a reaction, finally.

"So what do you talk about on first dates?" He finally glanced at her, eyes slowly scanning her face before turning back. Then he did a peculiar thing: sort of shuddered and made it look like he was clearing his throat.

"Oh," Caty cooed. "Why? Is this a first date?"

"No, no," he said, as if that were a silly idea. "I'm just asking since you were so against talking about your childhood."

"I'm not against it." Caty shrugged. "I'm just saying. Those are things you don't ask people right off the bat."

"But asking them if they've seen porn is?"

She widened her eyes, *Now there he is*. She's getting warmer. He's starting to show some personality, doing more than simply shaking his head, crossing his eyebrows, or snorting at her.

"Hey, I didn't ask. I just said," she clarified. "Everybody's seen porn. I absolutely won't believe it if you say you haven't."

Was that a shadow of a smile on his lips?

Caty kept her eyes on him. "What's your name again?"

The smile on his lips finally formed. It was reserved and polite, but a smile, still. "Elan."

"I'm Caty, by the way. In case you've forgotten by now and are too scared to ask again."

"I haven't," he snapped.

Caty leaned back. "Elan, huh? Where did that come from?"

"The dictionary," he answered flatly. So he was funny, after all. Caty felt herself smiling triumphantly for having coaxed a joke out of his polite-to-the-point-of-stuck-up exterior. "It's French. I think it means *enthusiasm* or something like that."

"Are you French?"

"Non," he answered.

"Ah, parlez-vous français?"

He paused. "I've been asked that question more than once, and sometimes I say, 'Oui,' and then I take it back."

"You shouldn't. You should keep faking it."

He shook his head. "I don't know any other French words."

"I can teach you," Caty offered. Sure, they only had a little time left, and they'd just met, but she could teach him a thing or two.

"You speak French?"

"A little bit. It was an elective at school. Not that I paid much attention. I visited Montreal a couple of times and learned the language better."

"So I take it you actually knew what my name meant?"

"Well," she answered. "No. I only speak tourist. I don't think élan is used in everyday conversations."

"Oh."

"I can teach you how to say important phrases, though."

"Like?"

"Voulez-vous coucher—"

"Alright," he cut her off. "I know what that means."

Caty cackled, "Good. I was testing you."

Elan gave her a look—one eyebrow arched—and something struck her about what he was doing. If he wasn't too careful, someone might confuse it with calculated seduction.

He couldn't be flirting with her, could he? That would be a weird turnaround of events considering how they started. They had been stumbling so badly and were now starting to find a rhythm.

"Je m'en fous," Caty coughed.

"What does that mean?"

"You have to say it first. Je m'en fous."

He pressed his lips together as if he was thinking about making an excuse not to do it, but he failed.

Caty laughed. "You don't have to look constipated. The French language is very sexy."

"And complicated. It's never spoken how it's spelled."

She rolled her eyes. "You don't seem to have a lot of élan today, Elan."

"Well," he sighed, "it's a tough name to live up to."

She laughed, more like a cackle. He was *really* funny, she decided, and she was finally starting to enjoy the ride.

"What about your name? Where did it come from?"

"Catalina," Caty answered with a wince. "Nothing special. My parents liked naming their kids after ancestors."

"It's also the name of a saint," he pointed out.

"I heard."

"She was a martyr."

Caty took a deep breath and sighed. "Well, look at that. We're both saddled with names we can't possibly live up to."

Elan threw her a glance, and she offered a quick smile.

"This is good." Caty nodded mostly to herself, adjusting her position on the seat. "Talking about the origins of our names, I'll keep it in mind as good first-date material."

"You get a lot of first dates?"

She found his question funny. "Sure. Don't you?"

"Not really."

Ah. Caty felt smug. So her theory about Elan not being the most popular person in school might be true. "I get why you're friends with Juliana now."

Andrews McMeel Publishing
a division of Andrews McMeel Universal
1130 Walnut Street, Kansas City, Missouri 64106

www.andrewsmcmeel.com

Contact the author: hello@dawnlanuza.com

19 20 21 22 23 RLP 10 9 8 7 6 5 4 3 2 1

ISBN: 978-1-4494-9756-9

Library of Congress Control Number: 2018951718

Editor: Patty Rice
Art Director: Holly Swayne
Production Editor: Elizabeth A. Garcia
Production Manager: Cliff Koehler

This book is a work of fiction. Names, characters, places, and incidents are products of the author's imagination or are used fictitiously. Any resemblance to actual events or locales or persons, living or dead, is entirely coincidental.

Attention: Schools and Businesses

Andrews McMeel books are available at quantity discounts with bulk purchase for educational, business, or sales promotional use. For information, please e-mail the Andrews McMeel Publishing Special Sales Department: specialsales@amuniversal.com.